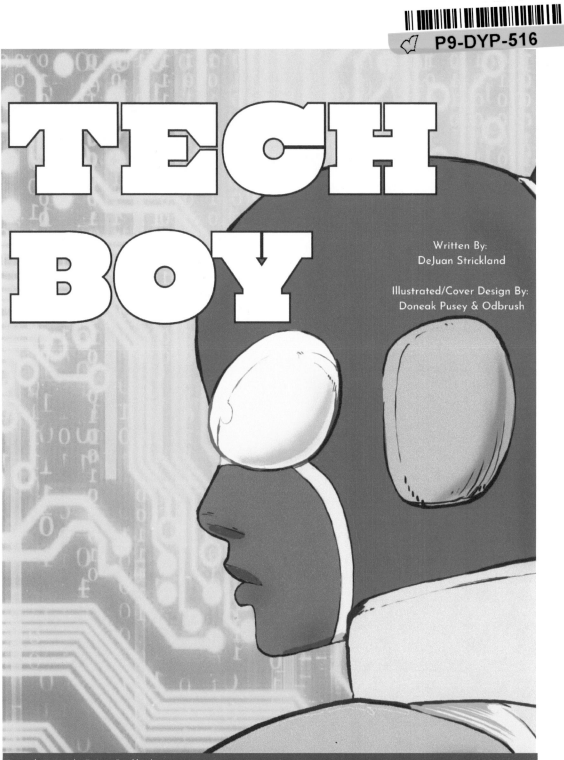

# TECH BOY

Written By:
DeJuan Strickland

Illustrated/Cover Design By:
Doneak Pusey & Odbrush

Printed in the United States of America
First Printing, 2021

Identifiers:
Library of Congress Control Number: 2021905884
ISBN (Paperback): 978-1-7369222-0-0
ISBN (eBook): 978-1-7369222-1-7

Published by DeJuan Strickland
St. Louis, MO
www.teamtechboy.com

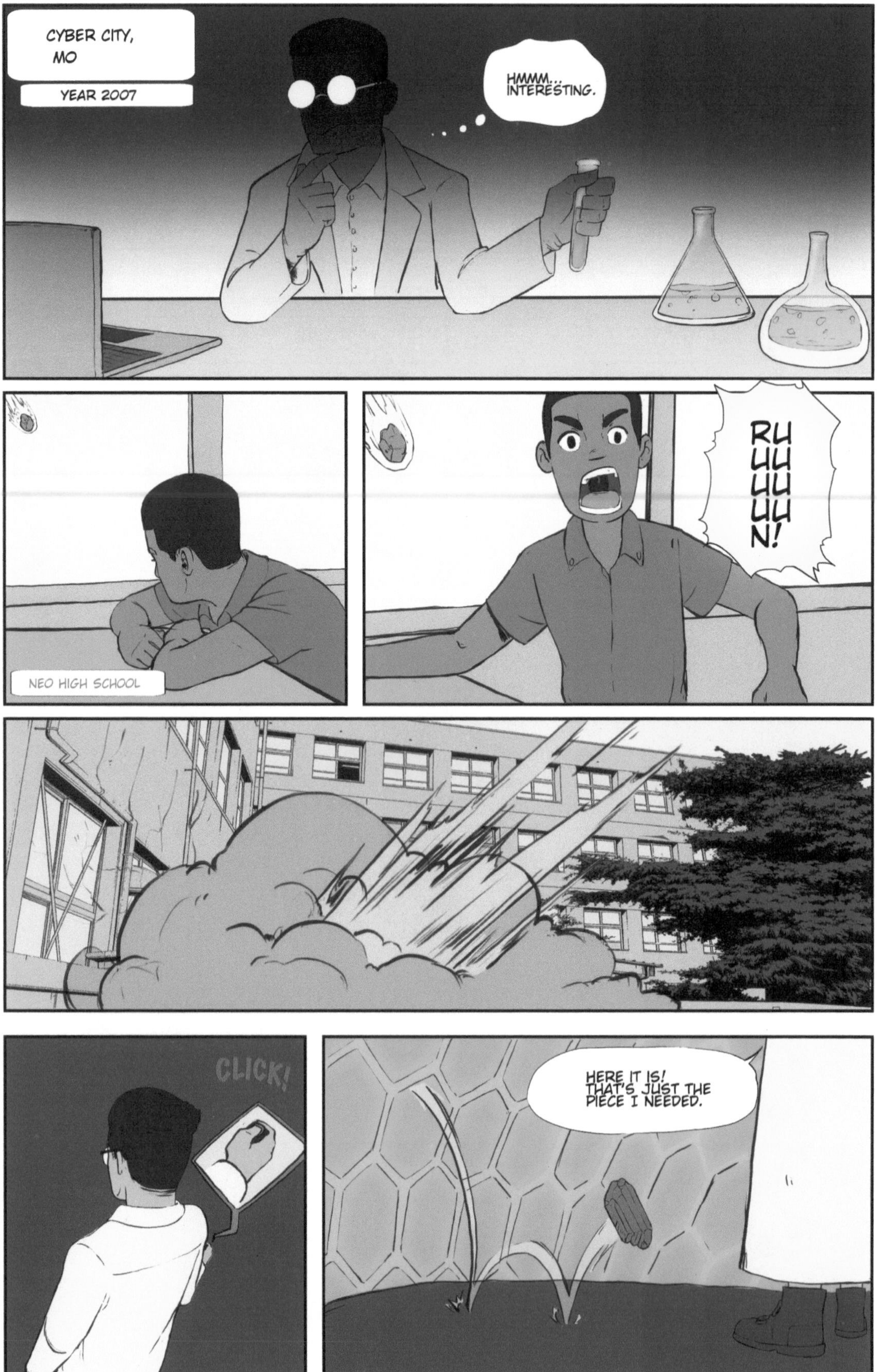
CYBER CITY, MO
YEAR 2007
HMMM... INTERESTING.
NEO HIGH SCHOOL
RUUUUUUN!
CLICK!
HERE IT IS! THAT'S JUST THE PIECE I NEEDED.

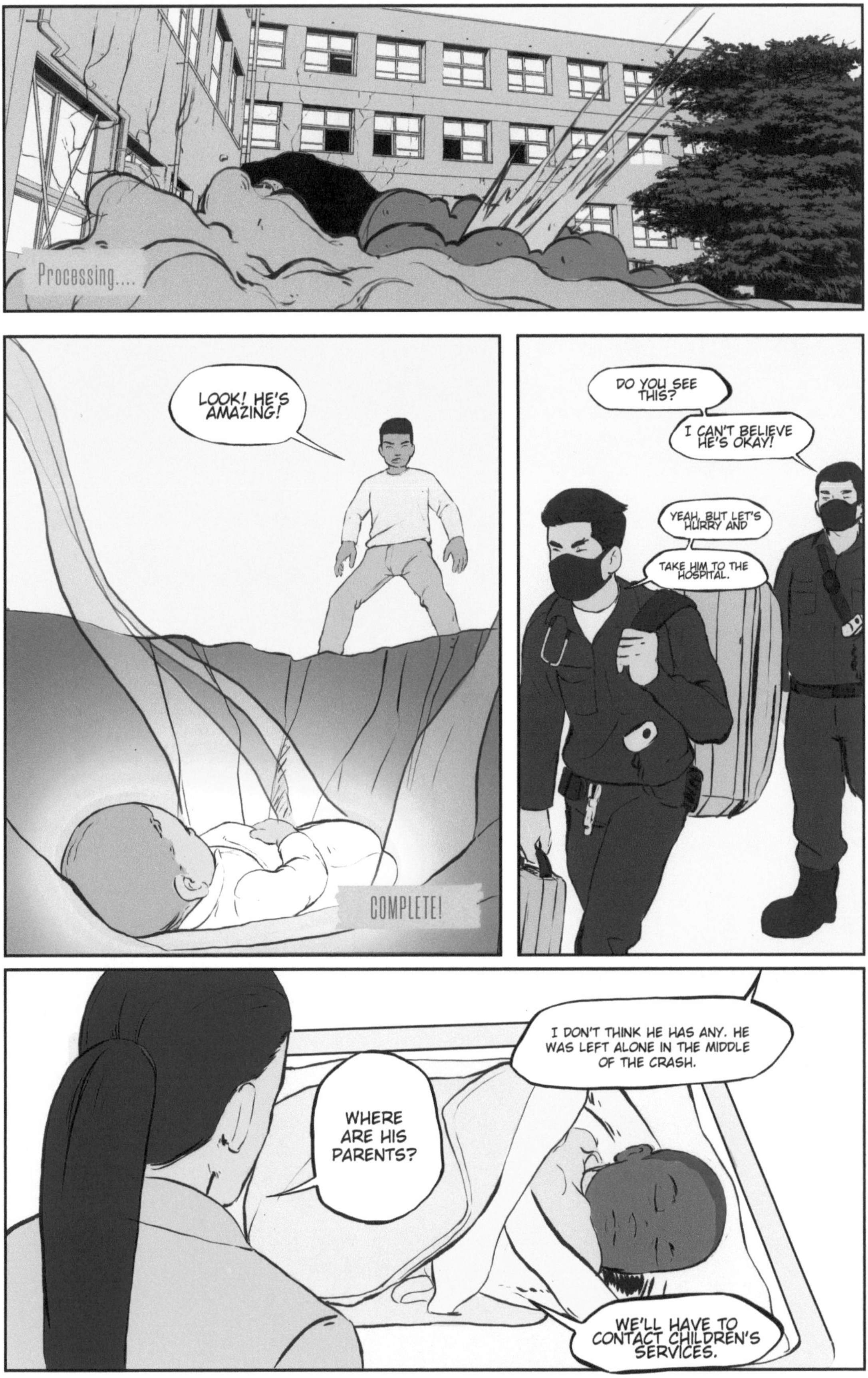
Processing....
LOOK! HE'S AMAZING!
COMPLETE!
DO YOU SEE THIS?
I CAN'T BELIEVE HE'S OKAY!
YEAH, BUT LET'S HURRY AND
TAKE HIM TO THE HOSPITAL.
WHERE ARE HIS PARENTS?
I DON'T THINK HE HAS ANY. HE WAS LEFT ALONE IN THE MIDDLE OF THE CRASH.
WE'LL HAVE TO CONTACT CHILDREN'S SERVICES.

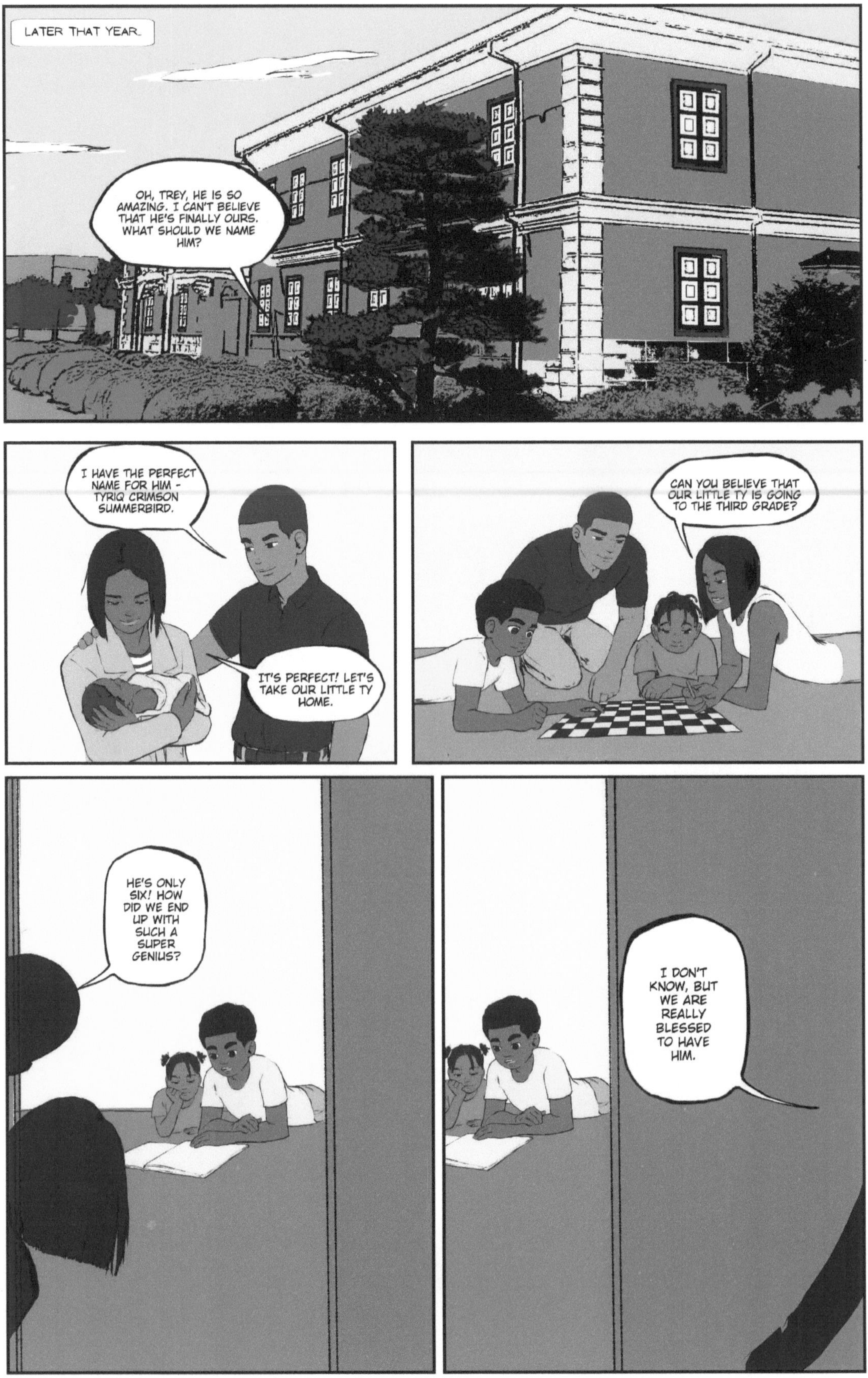
LATER THAT YEAR...
OH, TREY, HE IS SO AMAZING. I CAN'T BELIEVE THAT HE'S FINALLY OURS. WHAT SHOULD WE NAME HIM?
I HAVE THE PERFECT NAME FOR HIM - TYRIQ CRIMSON SUMMERBIRD.
IT'S PERFECT! LET'S TAKE OUR LITTLE TY HOME.
CAN YOU BELIEVE THAT OUR LITTLE TY IS GOING TO THE THIRD GRADE?
HE'S ONLY SIX! HOW DID WE END UP WITH SUCH A SUPER GENIUS?
I DON'T KNOW, BUT WE ARE REALLY BLESSED TO HAVE HIM.

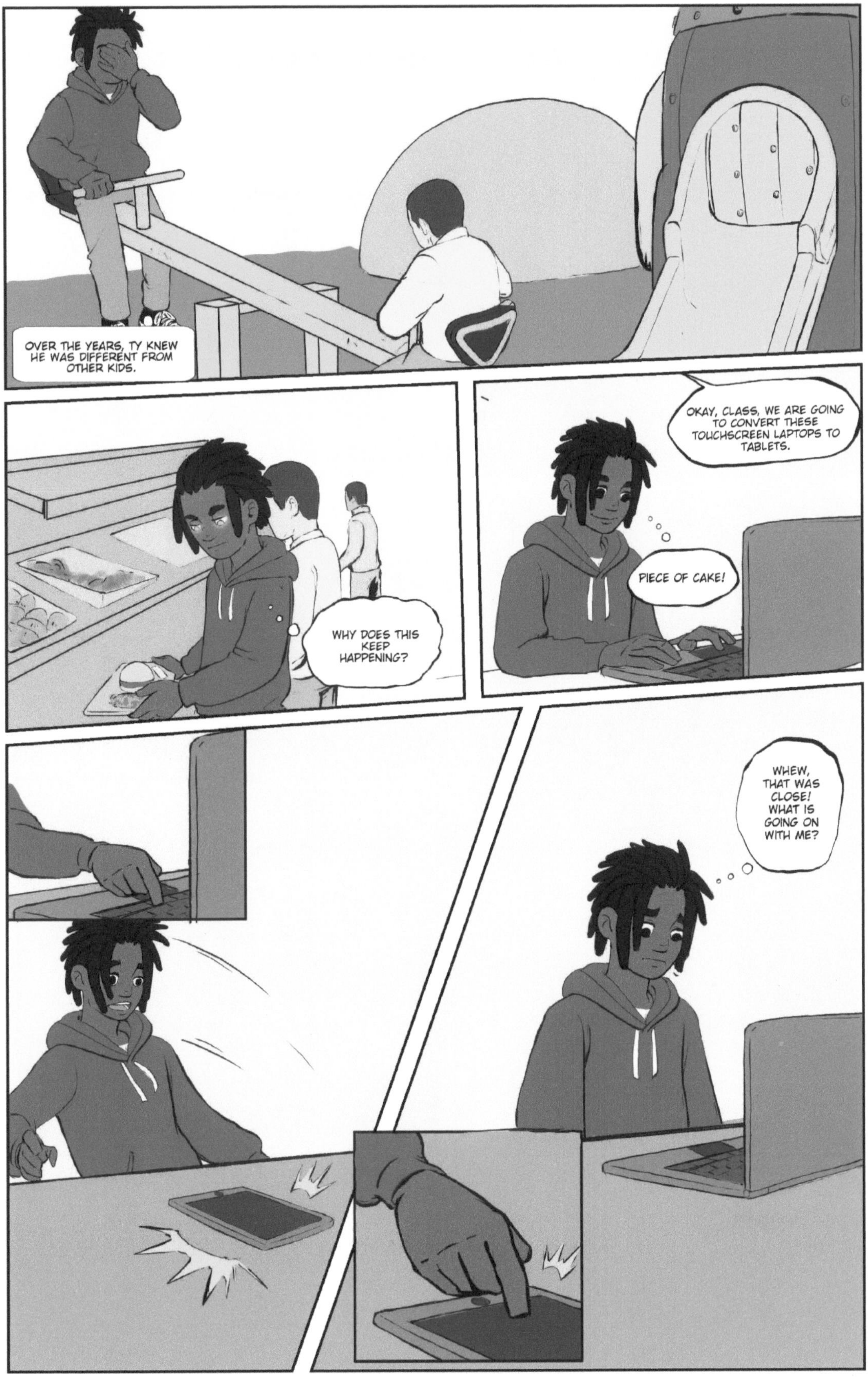
OVER THE YEARS, TY KNEW HE WAS DIFFERENT FROM OTHER KIDS.
WHY DOES THIS KEEP HAPPENING?
OKAY, CLASS, WE ARE GOING TO CONVERT THESE TOUCHSCREEN LAPTOPS TO TABLETS.
PIECE OF CAKE!
WHEW, THAT WAS CLOSE! WHAT IS GOING ON WITH ME?

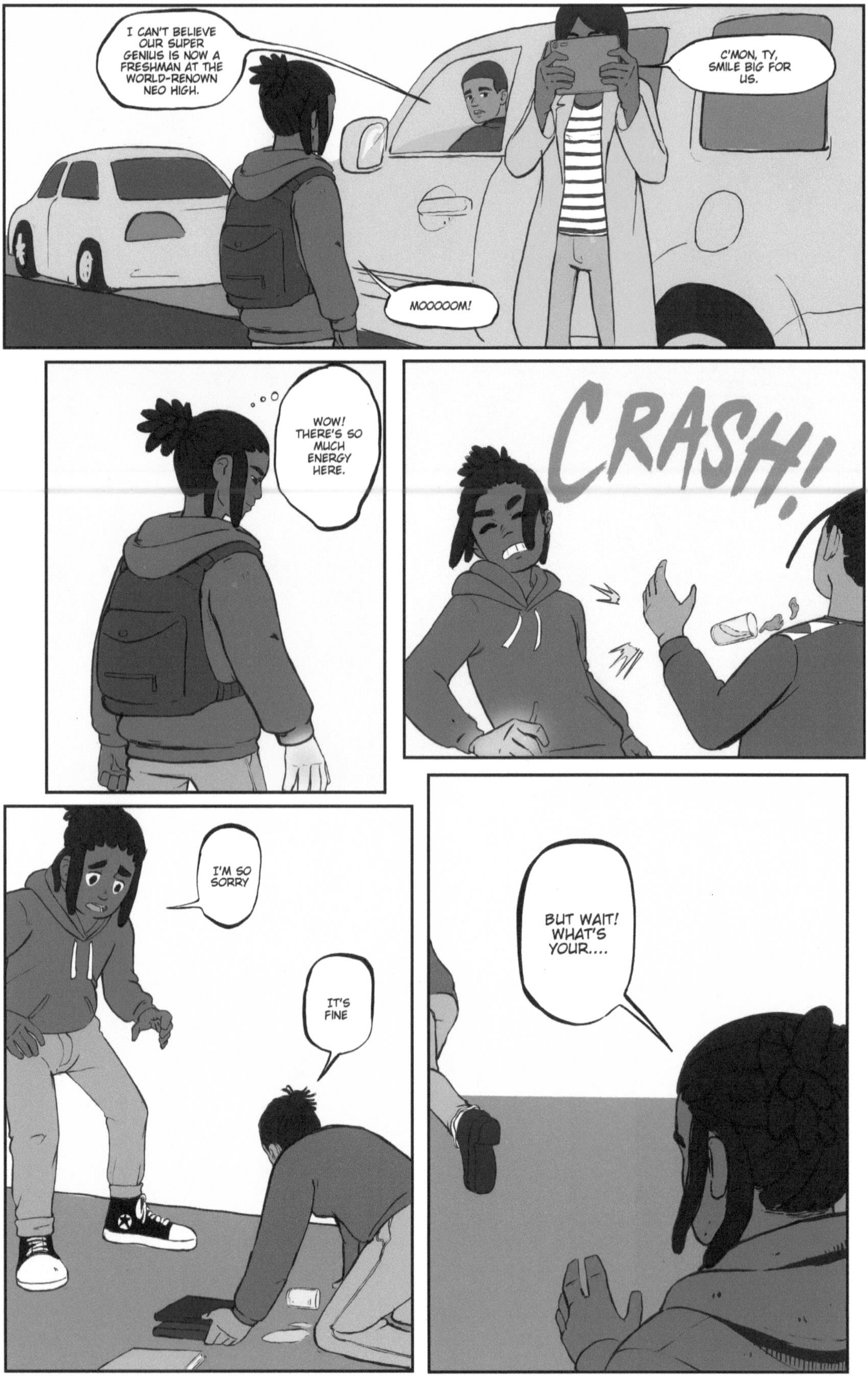
I CAN'T BELIEVE OUR SUPER GENIUS IS NOW A FRESHMAN AT THE WORLD-RENOWN NEO HIGH.
C'MON, TY, SMILE BIG FOR US.
MOOOOOM!
WOW! THERE'S SO MUCH ENERGY HERE.
CRASH!
I'M SO SORRY
IT'S FINE
BUT WAIT! WHAT'S YOUR....

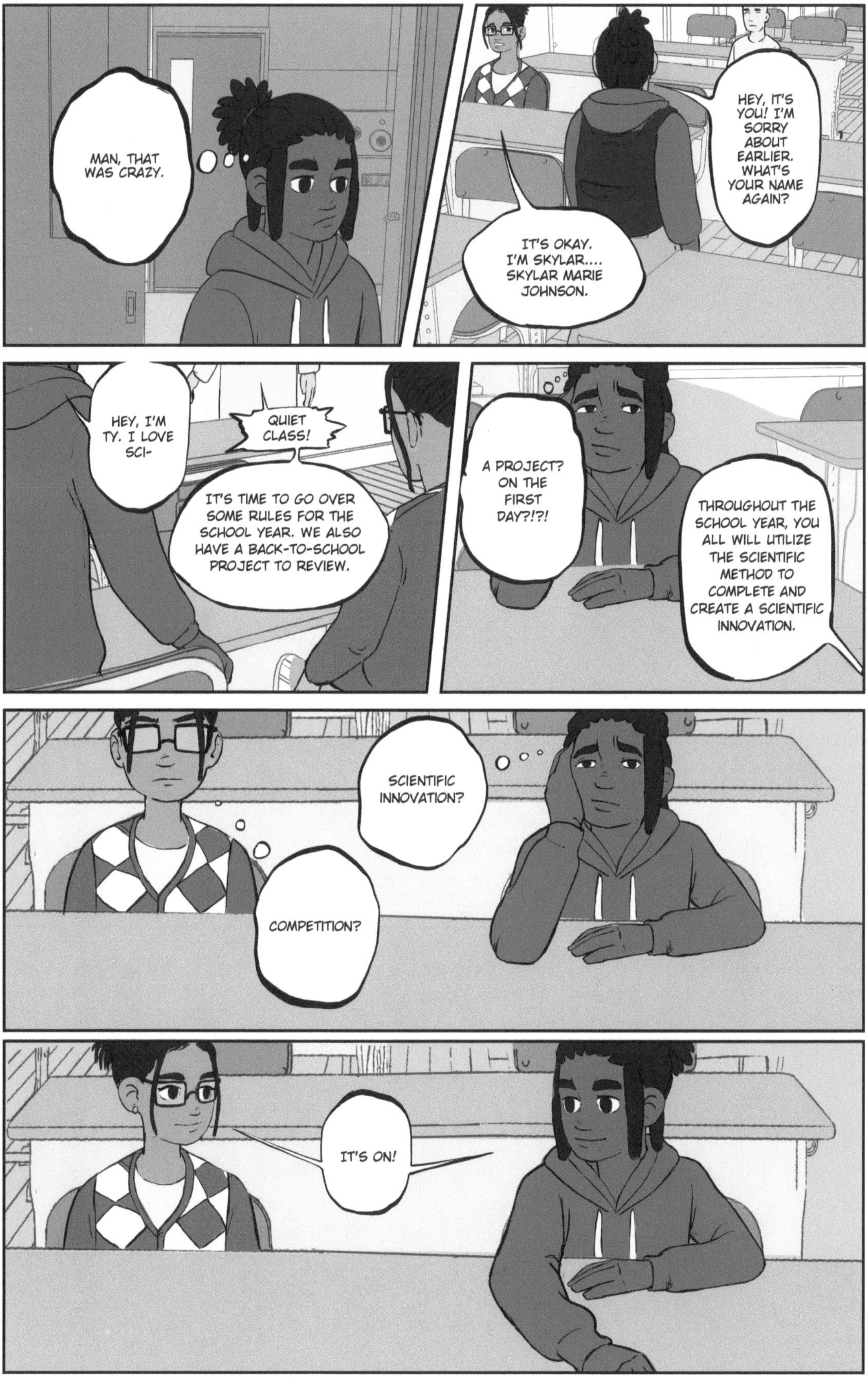
MAN, THAT WAS CRAZY.
HEY, IT'S YOU! I'M SORRY ABOUT EARLIER. WHAT'S YOUR NAME AGAIN?
IT'S OKAY. I'M SKYLAR.... SKYLAR MARIE JOHNSON.
HEY, I'M TY. I LOVE SCI-
QUIET CLASS!
IT'S TIME TO GO OVER SOME RULES FOR THE SCHOOL YEAR. WE ALSO HAVE A BACK-TO-SCHOOL PROJECT TO REVIEW.
A PROJECT? ON THE FIRST DAY?!?!
THROUGHOUT THE SCHOOL YEAR, YOU ALL WILL UTILIZE THE SCIENTIFIC METHOD TO COMPLETE AND CREATE A SCIENTIFIC INNOVATION.
SCIENTIFIC INNOVATION?
COMPETITION?
IT'S ON!

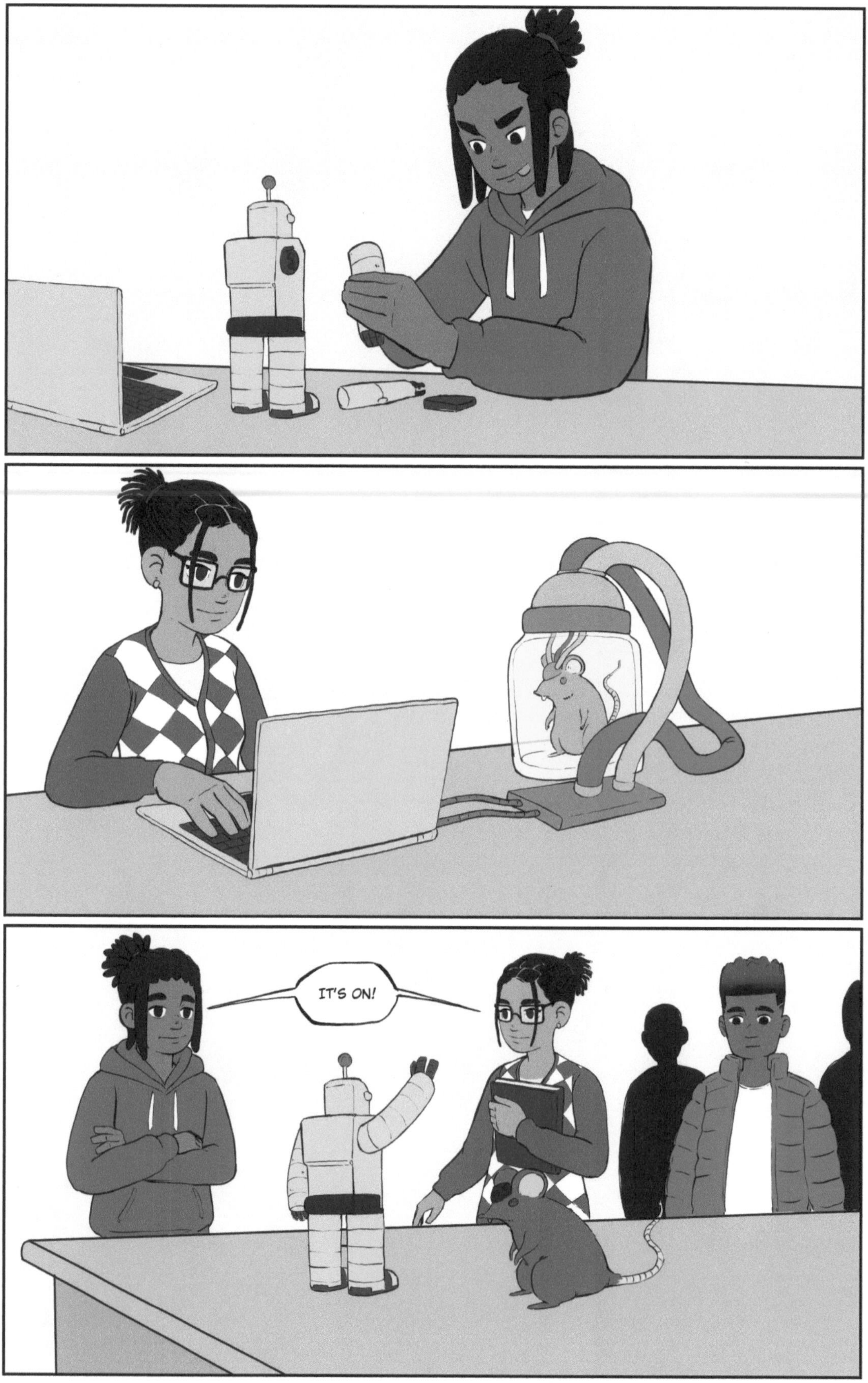
IT'S ON!

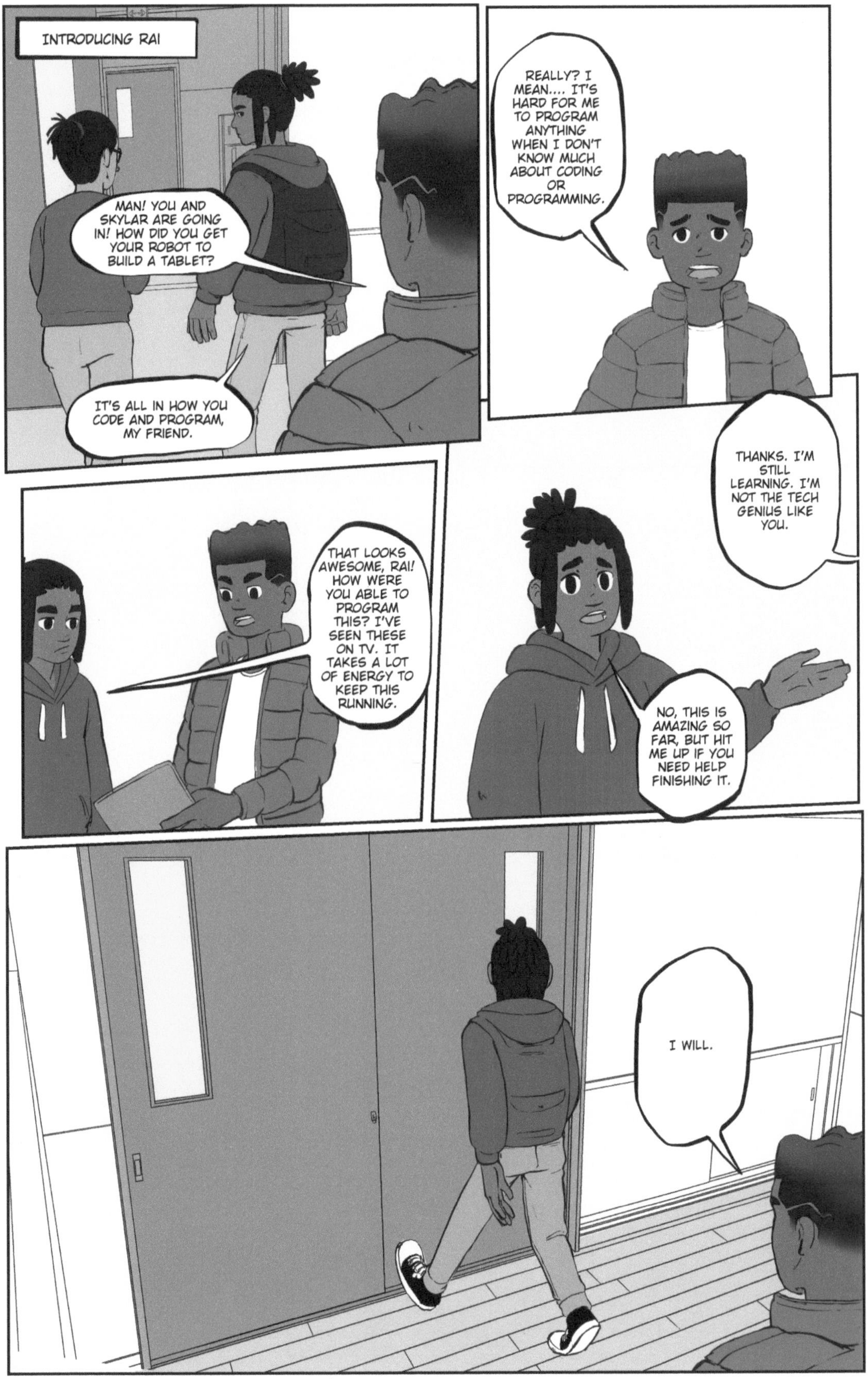
INTRODUCING RAI
MAN! YOU AND SKYLAR ARE GOING IN! HOW DID YOU GET YOUR ROBOT TO BUILD A TABLET?
IT'S ALL IN HOW YOU CODE AND PROGRAM, MY FRIEND.
REALLY? I MEAN.... IT'S HARD FOR ME TO PROGRAM ANYTHING WHEN I DON'T KNOW MUCH ABOUT CODING OR PROGRAMMING.
THAT LOOKS AWESOME, RAI! HOW WERE YOU ABLE TO PROGRAM THIS? I'VE SEEN THESE ON TV. IT TAKES A LOT OF ENERGY TO KEEP THIS RUNNING.
THANKS. I'M STILL LEARNING. I'M NOT THE TECH GENIUS LIKE YOU.
NO, THIS IS AMAZING SO FAR, BUT HIT ME UP IF YOU NEED HELP FINISHING IT.
I WILL.

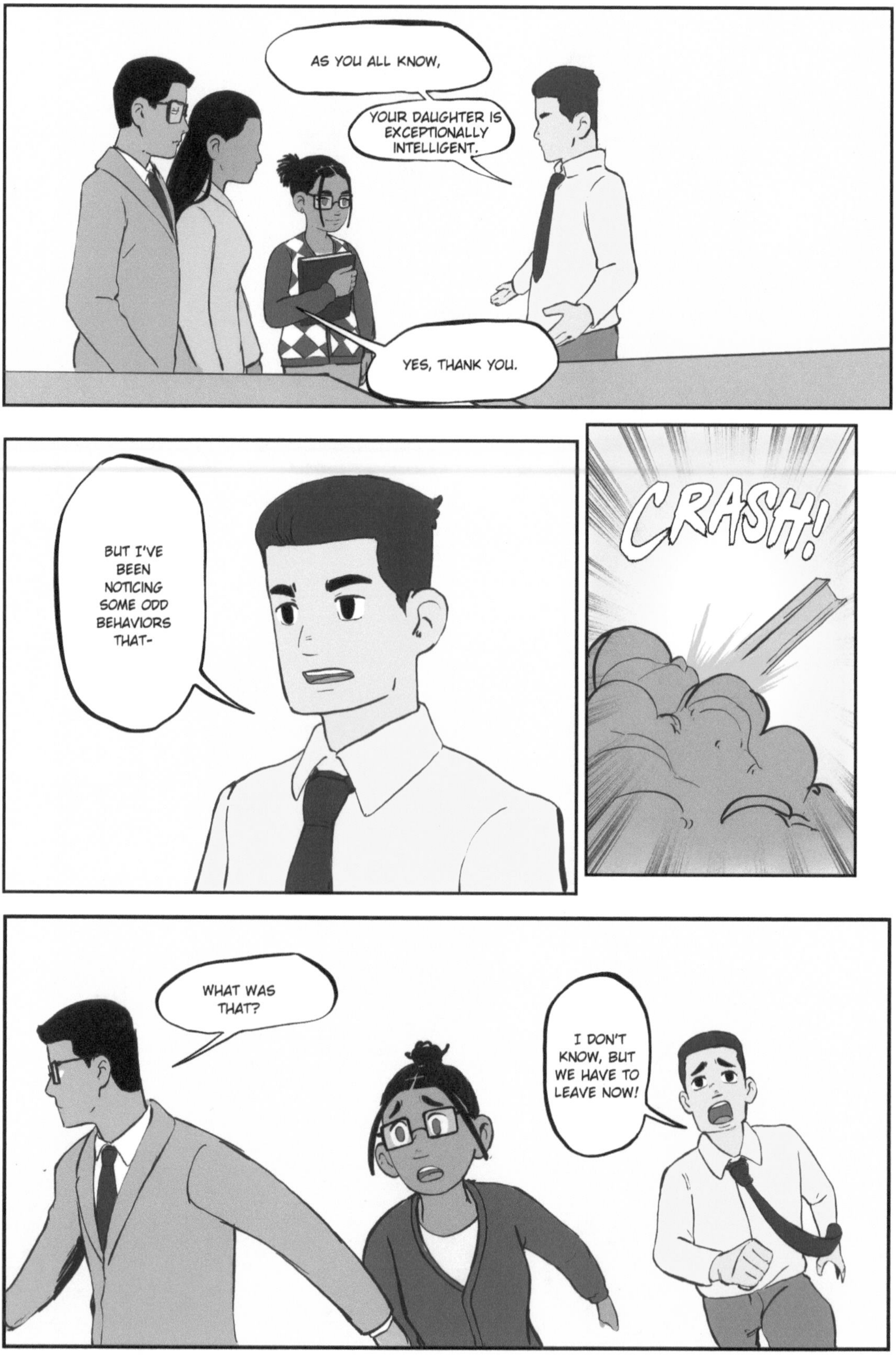
AS YOU ALL KNOW,
YOUR DAUGHTER IS EXCEPTIONALLY INTELLIGENT.
YES, THANK YOU.
BUT I'VE BEEN NOTICING SOME ODD BEHAVIORS THAT-
CRASH!
WHAT WAS THAT?
I DON'T KNOW, BUT WE HAVE TO LEAVE NOW!

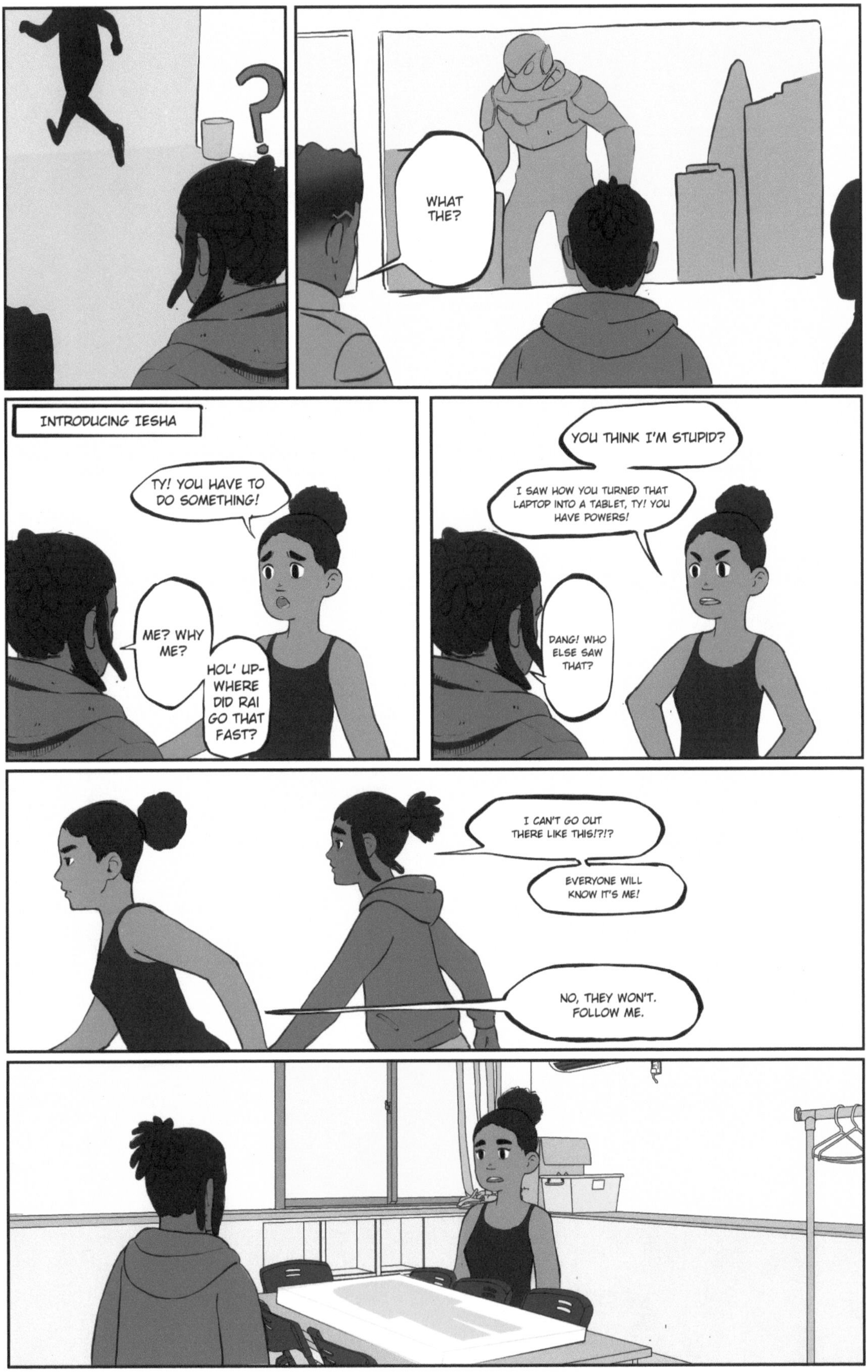
?
WHAT THE?
INTRODUCING IESHA
TY! YOU HAVE TO DO SOMETHING!
ME? WHY ME?
HOL' UP- WHERE DID RAI GO THAT FAST?
YOU THINK I'M STUPID?
I SAW HOW YOU TURNED THAT LAPTOP INTO A TABLET, TY! YOU HAVE POWERS!
DANG! WHO ELSE SAW THAT?
I CAN'T GO OUT THERE LIKE THIS!?!?
EVERYONE WILL KNOW IT'S ME!
NO, THEY WON'T. FOLLOW ME.

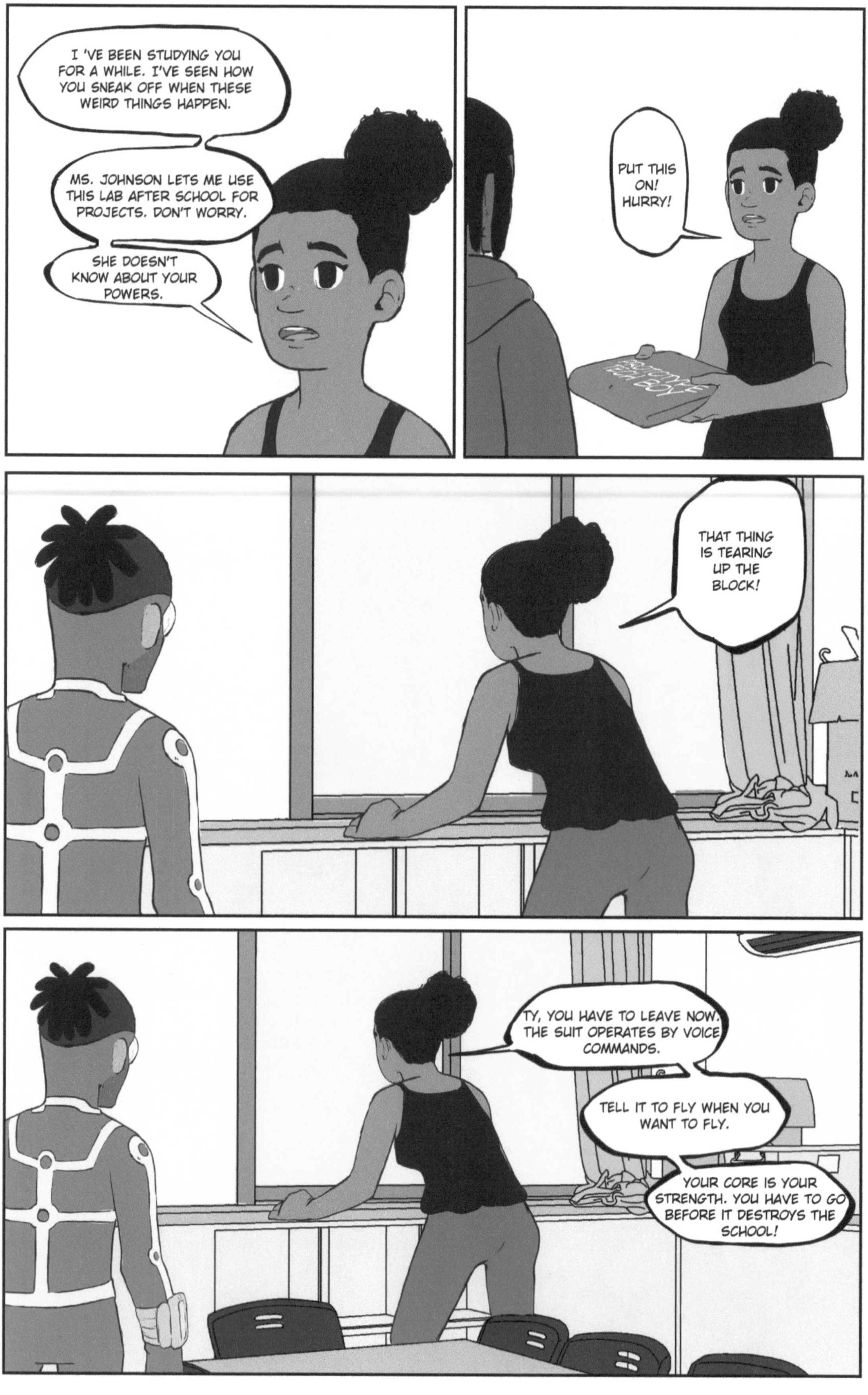
I 'VE BEEN STUDYING YOU FOR A WHILE. I'VE SEEN HOW YOU SNEAK OFF WHEN THESE WEIRD THINGS HAPPEN.
MS. JOHNSON LETS ME USE THIS LAB AFTER SCHOOL FOR PROJECTS. DON'T WORRY.
SHE DOESN'T KNOW ABOUT YOUR POWERS.
PUT THIS ON! HURRY!
THAT THING IS TEARING UP THE BLOCK!
TY, YOU HAVE TO LEAVE NOW. THE SUIT OPERATES BY VOICE COMMANDS.
TELL IT TO FLY WHEN YOU WANT TO FLY.
YOUR CORE IS YOUR STRENGTH. YOU HAVE TO GO BEFORE IT DESTROYS THE SCHOOL!

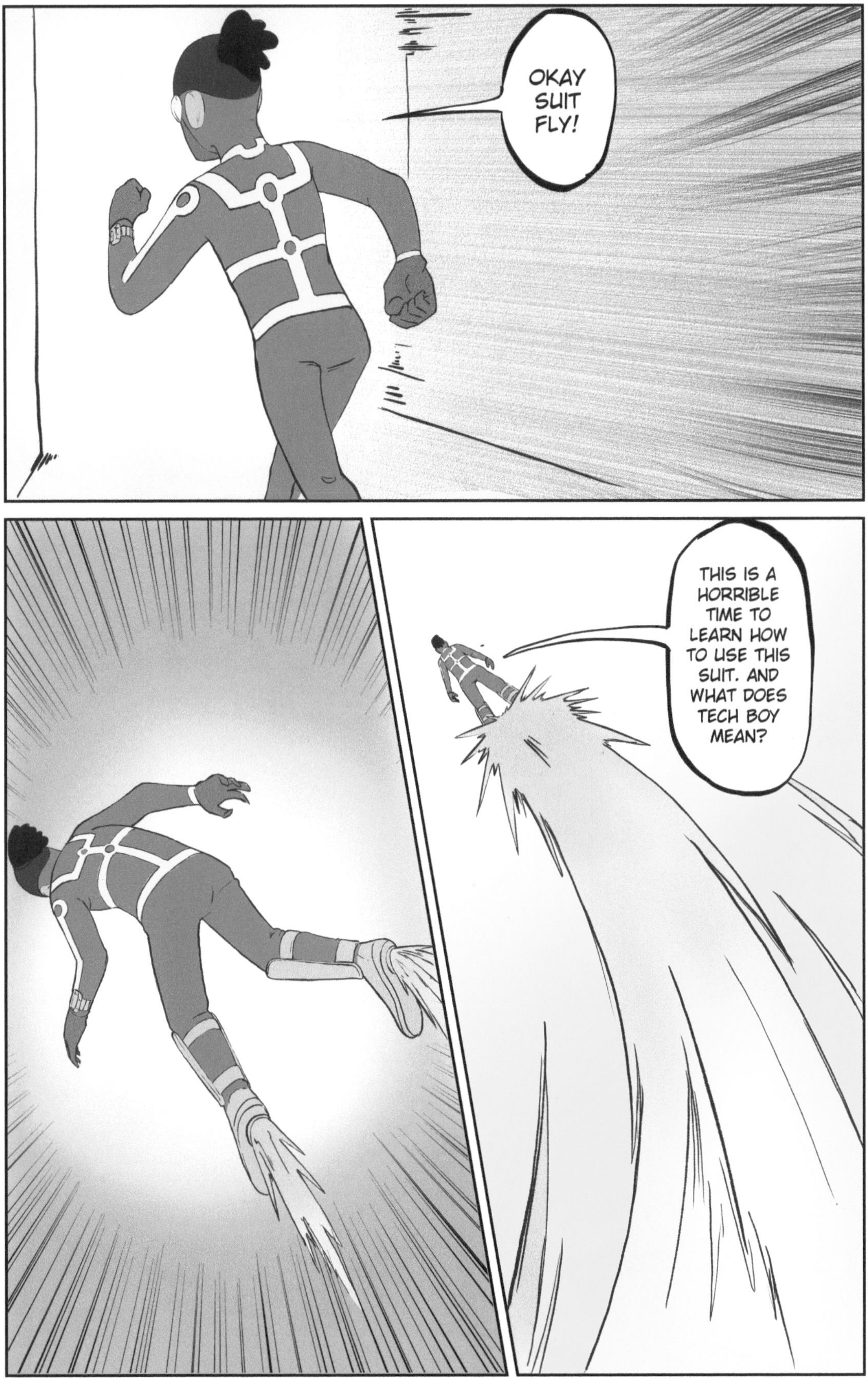
OKAY SUIT FLY!
THIS IS A HORRIBLE TIME TO LEARN HOW TO USE THIS SUIT. AND WHAT DOES TECH BOY MEAN?

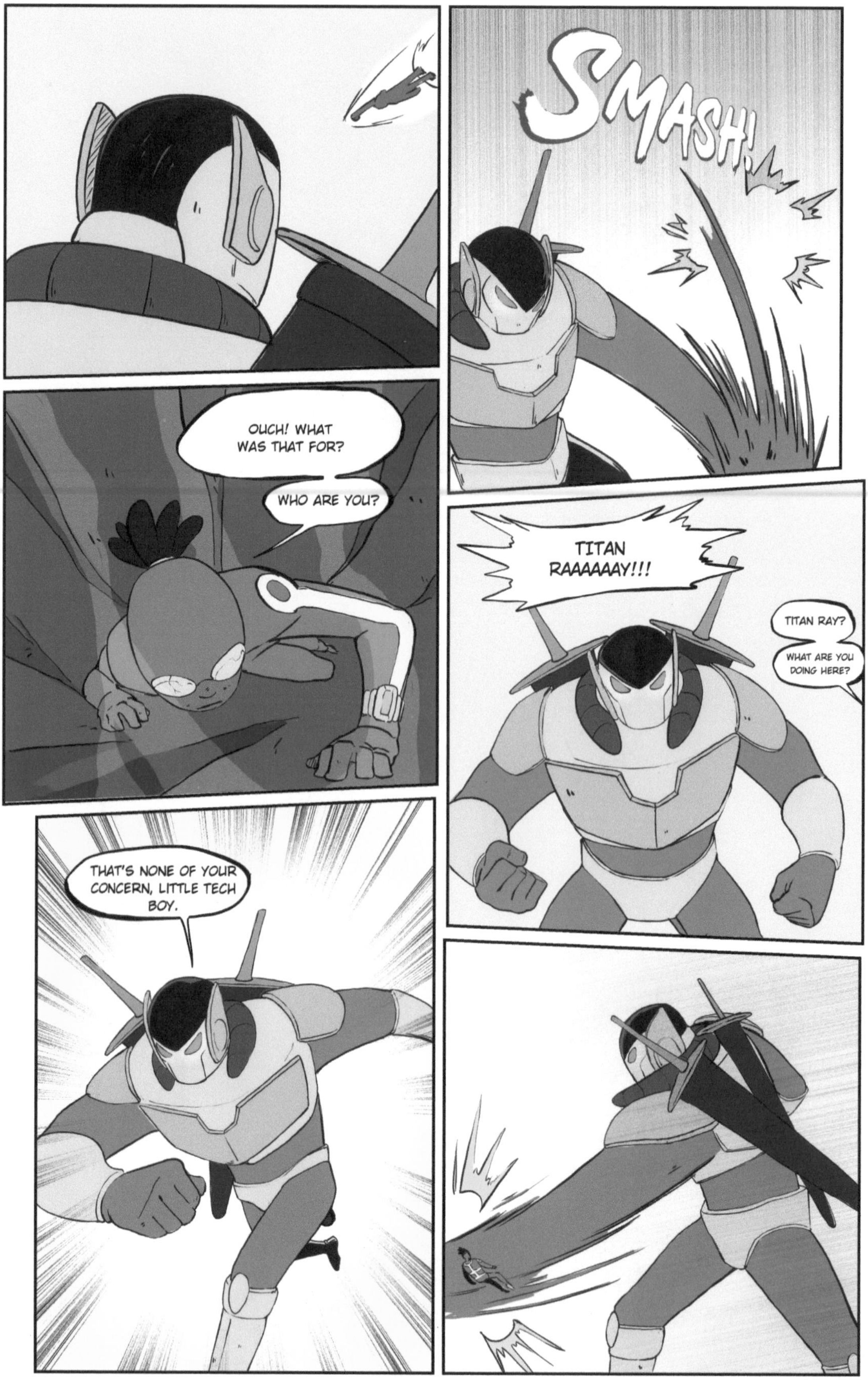
SMASH!
OUCH! WHAT WAS THAT FOR?
WHO ARE YOU?
TITAN RAAAAAAY!!!
TITAN RAY?
WHAT ARE YOU DOING HERE?
THAT'S NONE OF YOUR CONCERN, LITTLE TECH BOY.

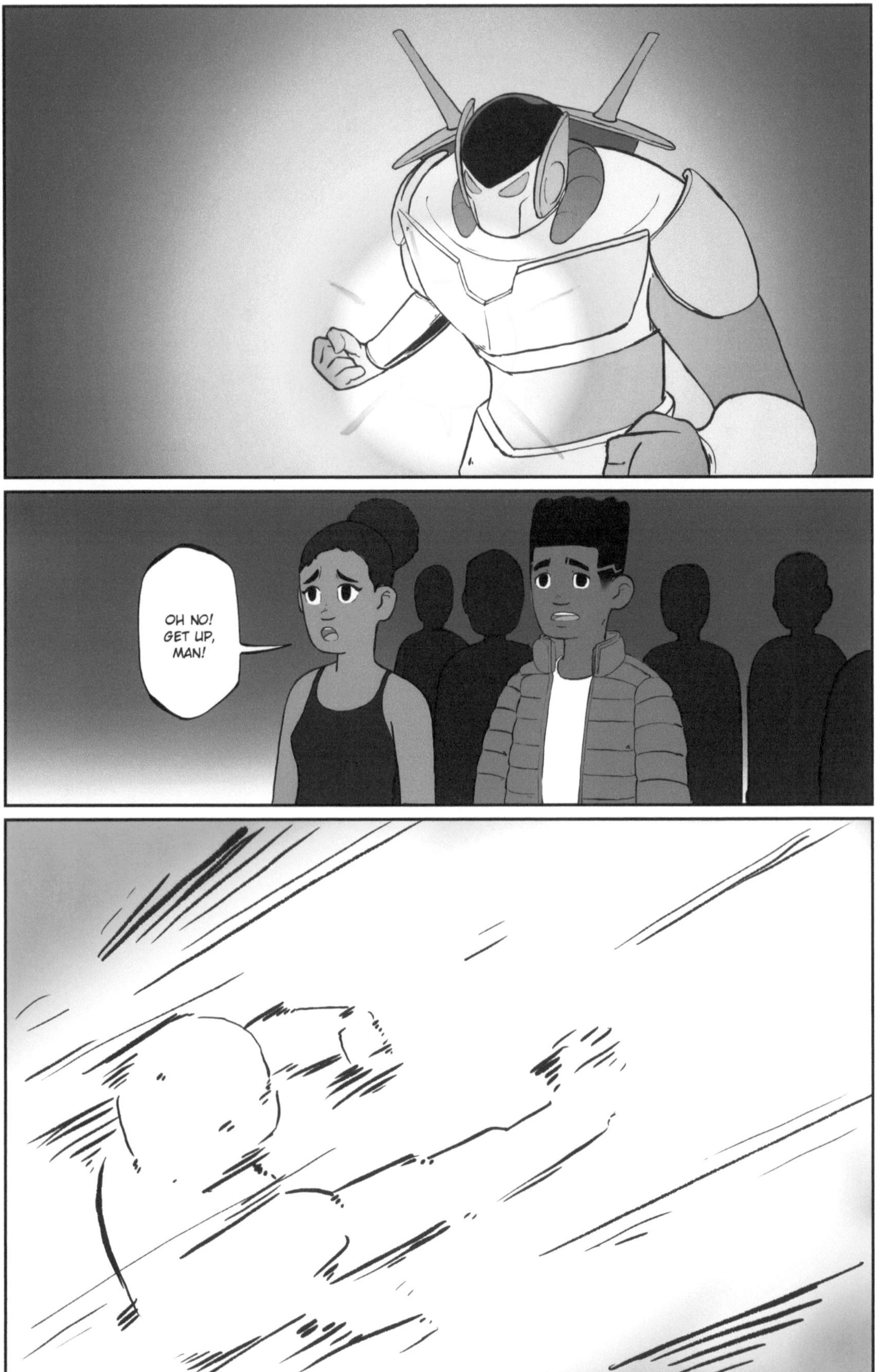
OH NO! GET UP, MAN!

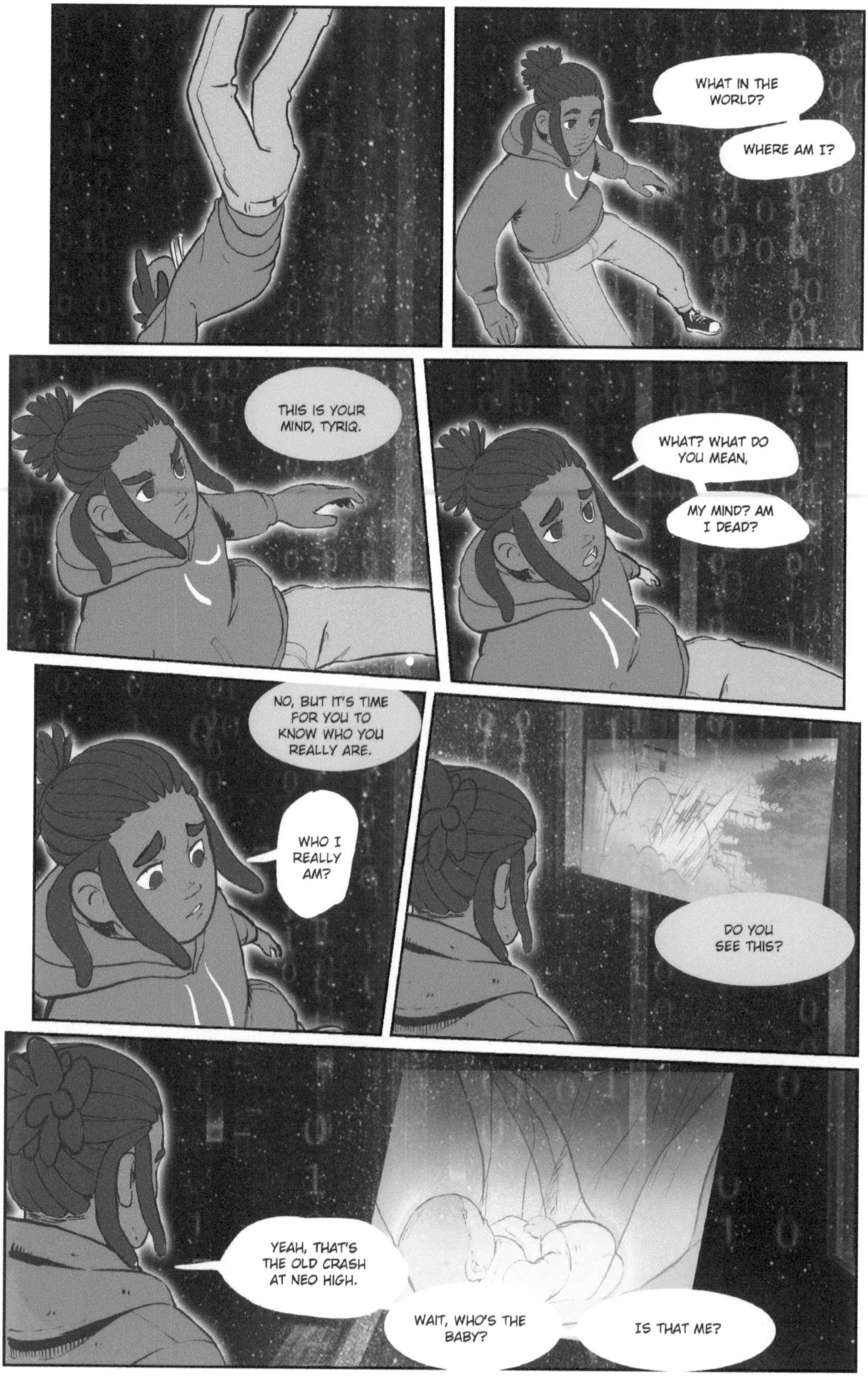
WHAT IN THE WORLD?
WHERE AM I?
THIS IS YOUR MIND, TYRIQ.
WHAT? WHAT DO YOU MEAN,
MY MIND? AM I DEAD?
NO, BUT IT'S TIME FOR YOU TO KNOW WHO YOU REALLY ARE.
WHO I REALLY AM?
DO YOU SEE THIS?
YEAH, THAT'S THE OLD CRASH AT NEO HIGH.
WAIT, WHO'S THE BABY?
IS THAT ME?

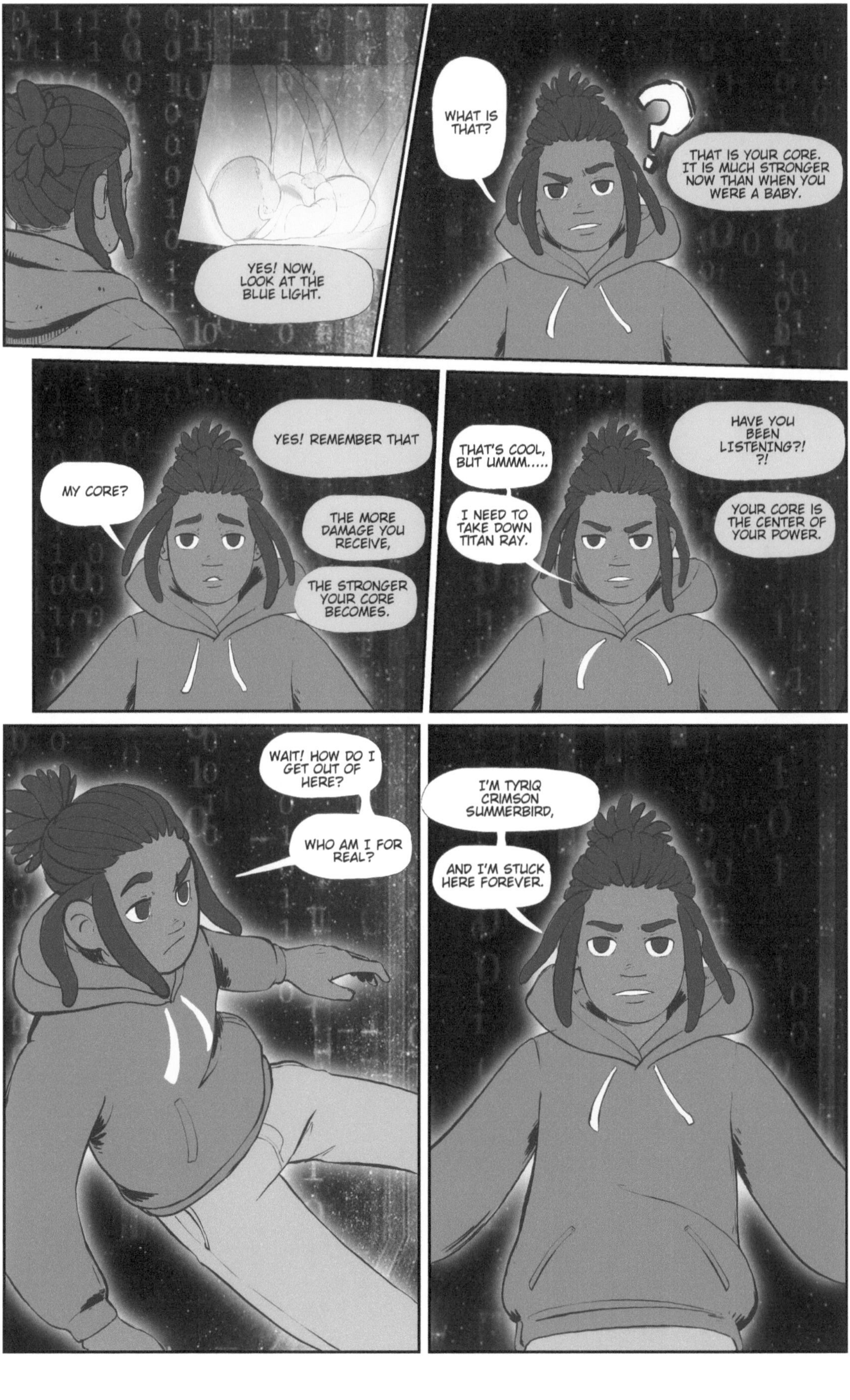
YES! NOW, LOOK AT THE BLUE LIGHT.
WHAT IS THAT?
THAT IS YOUR CORE. IT IS MUCH STRONGER NOW THAN WHEN YOU WERE A BABY.
YES! REMEMBER THAT
MY CORE?
THE MORE DAMAGE YOU RECEIVE,
THE STRONGER YOUR CORE BECOMES.
HAVE YOU BEEN LISTENING?! ?!
THAT'S COOL, BUT UMMM.....
I NEED TO TAKE DOWN TITAN RAY.
YOUR CORE IS THE CENTER OF YOUR POWER.
WAIT! HOW DO I GET OUT OF HERE?
WHO AM I FOR REAL?
I'M TYRIQ CRIMSON SUMMERBIRD,
AND I'M STUCK HERE FOREVER.

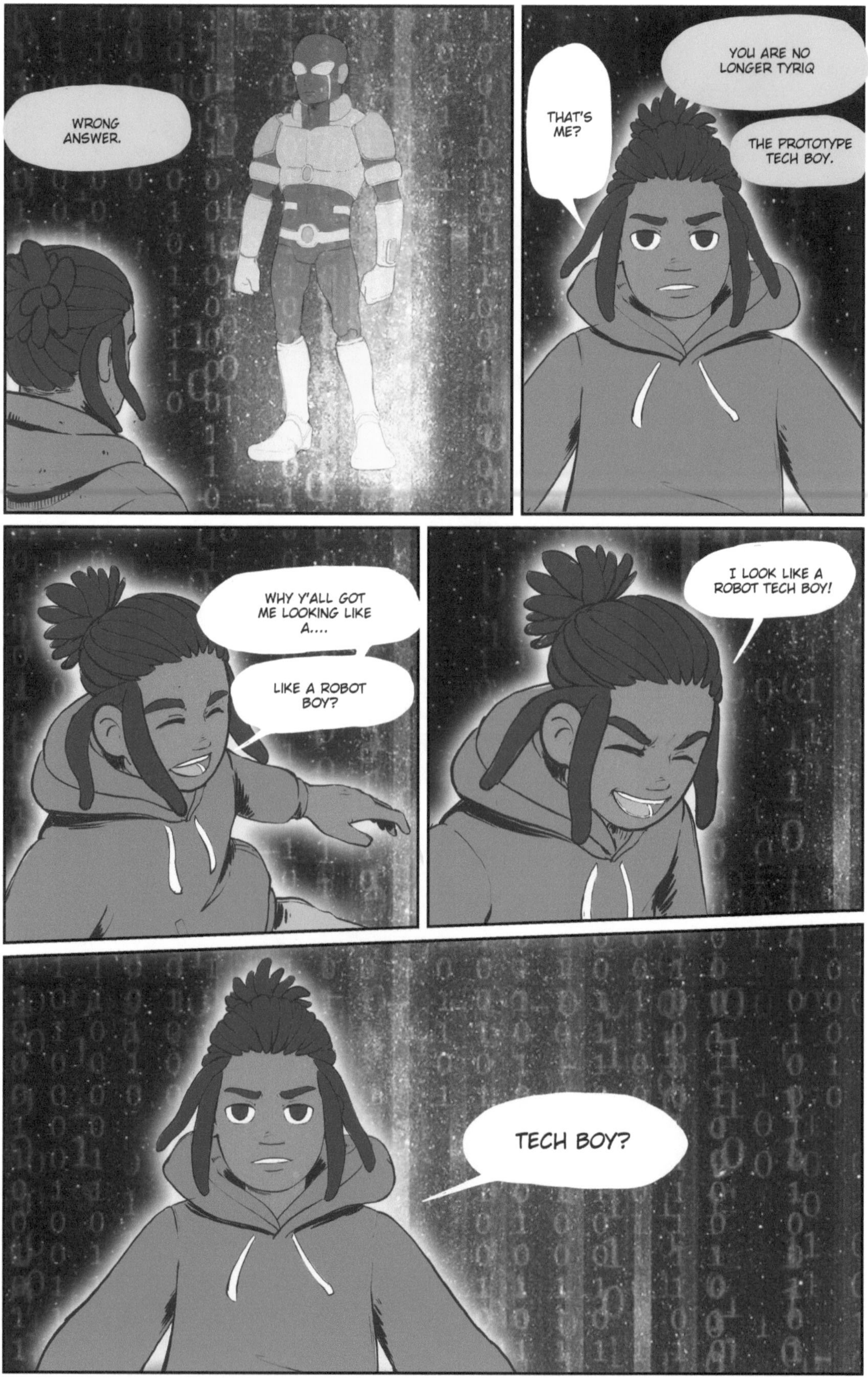
WRONG ANSWER.
YOU ARE NO LONGER TYRIQ
THAT'S ME?
THE PROTOTYPE TECH BOY.
WHY Y'ALL GOT ME LOOKING LIKE A....
LIKE A ROBOT BOY?
I LOOK LIKE A ROBOT TECH BOY!
TECH BOY?

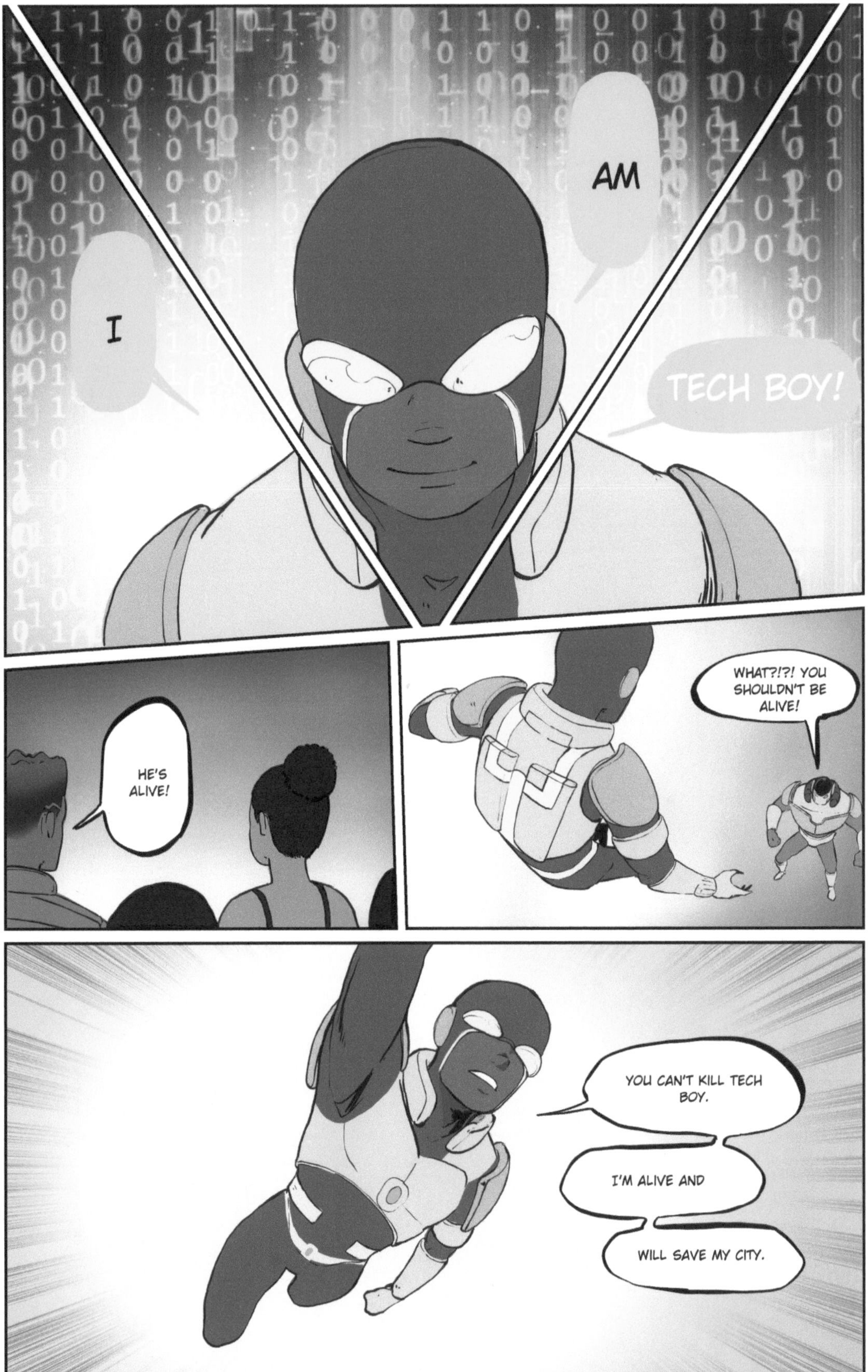
I
AM
TECH BOY!
HE'S ALIVE!
WHAT?!?! YOU SHOULDN'T BE ALIVE!
YOU CAN'T KILL TECH BOY.
I'M ALIVE AND
WILL SAVE MY CITY.

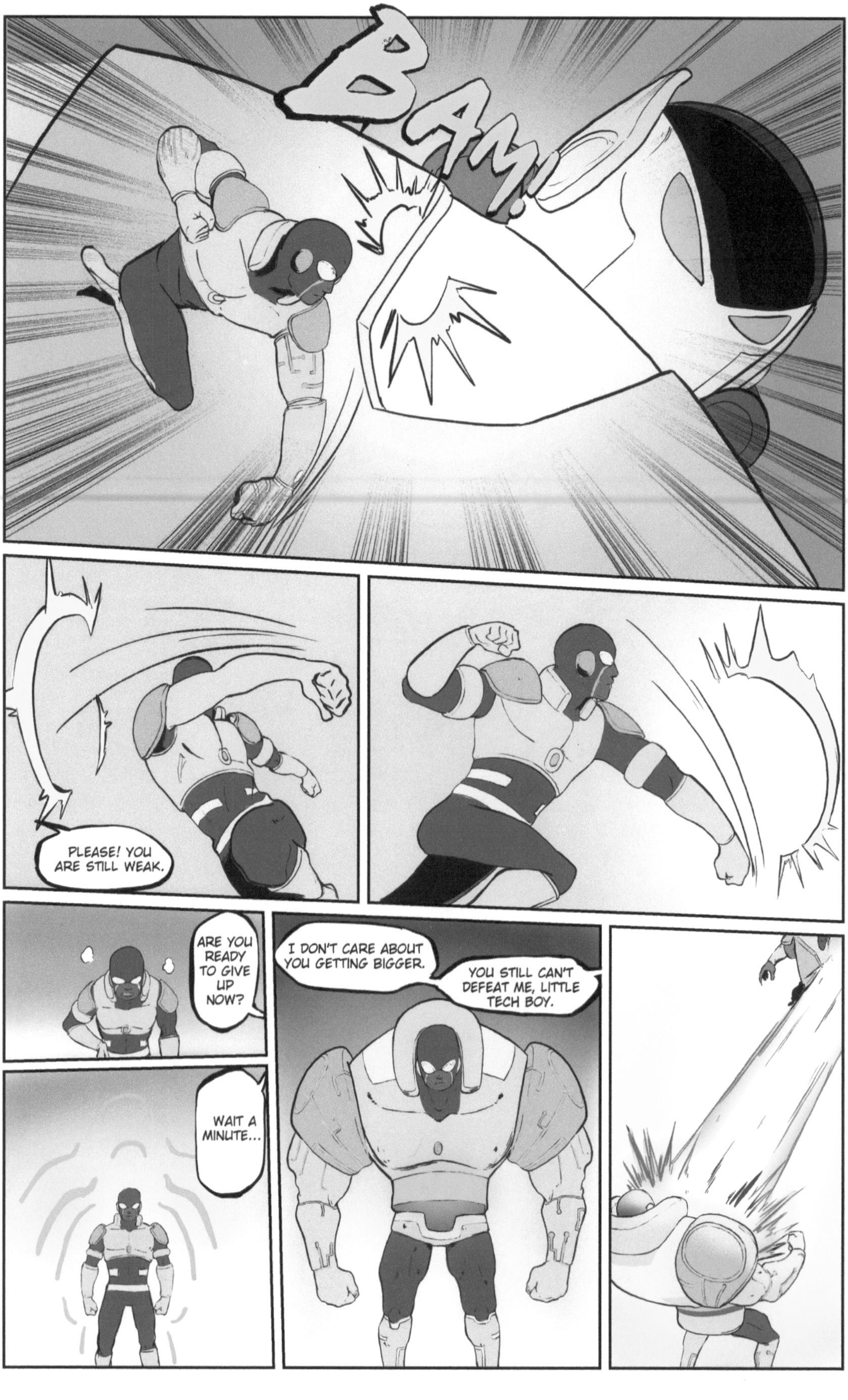
BAM!!
PLEASE! YOU ARE STILL WEAK.
ARE YOU READY TO GIVE UP NOW?
WAIT A MINUTE...
I DON'T CARE ABOUT YOU GETTING BIGGER.
YOU STILL CAN'T DEFEAT ME, LITTLE TECH BOY.

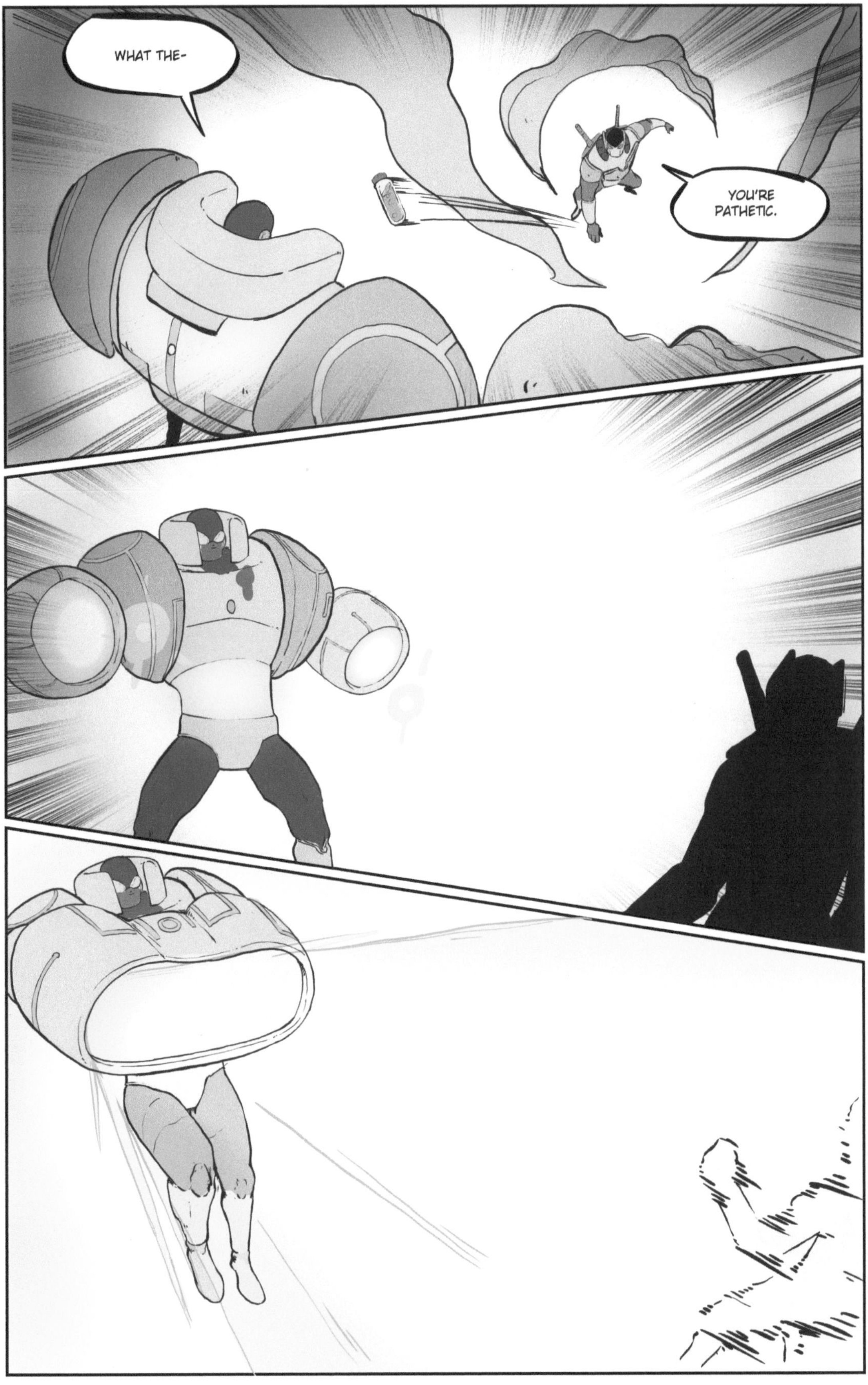
WHAT THE-
YOU'RE PATHETIC.

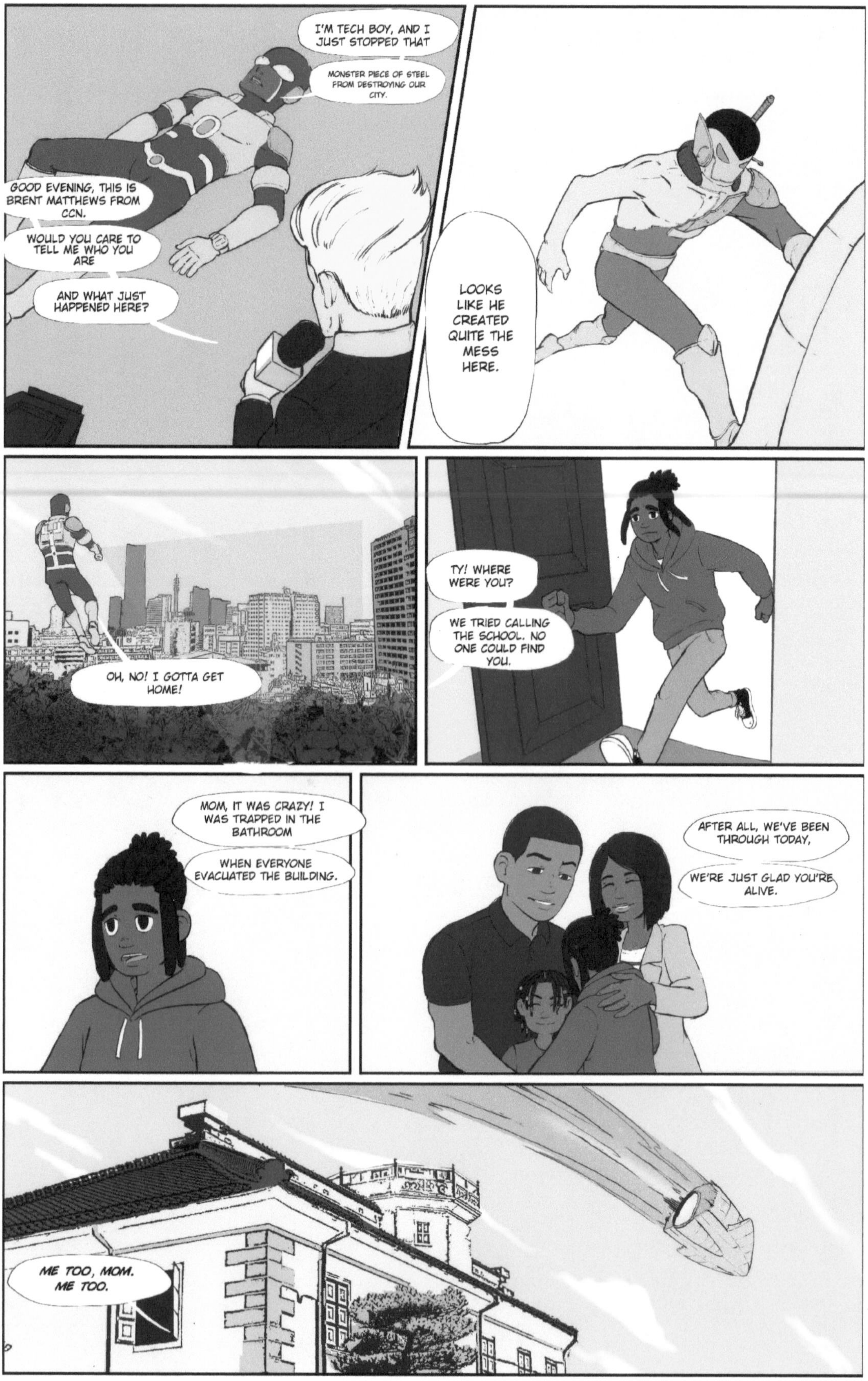
I'M TECH BOY, AND I JUST STOPPED THAT
MONSTER PIECE OF STEEL FROM DESTROYING OUR CITY.
GOOD EVENING, THIS IS BRENT MATTHEWS FROM CCN.
WOULD YOU CARE TO TELL ME WHO YOU ARE
AND WHAT JUST HAPPENED HERE?
LOOKS LIKE HE CREATED QUITE THE MESS HERE.
OH, NO! I GOTTA GET HOME!
TY! WHERE WERE YOU?
WE TRIED CALLING THE SCHOOL. NO ONE COULD FIND YOU.
MOM, IT WAS CRAZY! I WAS TRAPPED IN THE BATHROOM
WHEN EVERYONE EVACUATED THE BUILDING.
AFTER ALL, WE'VE BEEN THROUGH TODAY,
WE'RE JUST GLAD YOU'RE ALIVE.
ME TOO, MOM. ME TOO.

# ABOUT THE AUTHOR

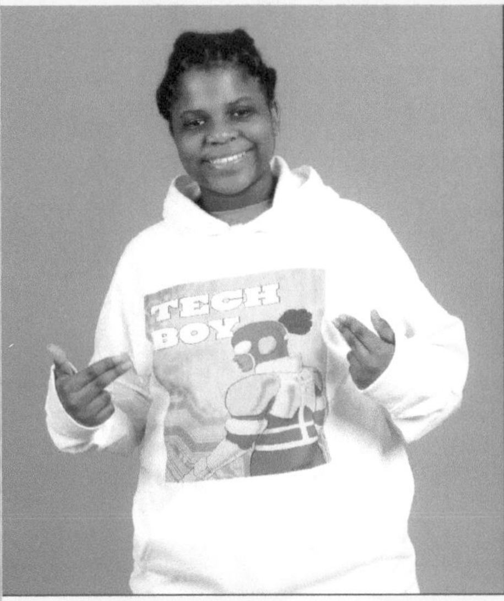
TECH
BOY

DEJUAN STRICKLAND IS A 12-YEAR-OLD SCHOLAR BORN AND RAISED IN ST. LOUIS, MISSOURI. HE ENJOYS GAMING, ANIME, READING, AND INDULGING IN COMIC BOOKS. HE IS A LONG-TIME HONOR ROLL STUDENT WHO THOROUGHLY ENJOYS SCIENCE AND TECHNOLOGY. HE HAS RECENTLY BEEN APPOINTED AS A YOUTH MEMBER OF STEMSTL'S STRATEGIC ADVISORY BOARD. HIS MISSION FOR TECH BOY IS TO INSPIRE OTHER YOUTH TO BECOME TECH-SAVVY ENTREPRENEURS.

## TECH BOY WAS WRITTEN IN HONOR OF MY REAL-LIFE SUPERHERO, CHADWICK BOSEMAN. THANK YOU FOR USING YOUR EXTRAORDINARY TALENT TO ENCOURAGE AND UPLIFT OTHERS.

CODING IS AN INTRIGUING AREA IN THE WORLD OF TECHNOLOGY. ACCORDING TO CONNECTED LEARNING ALLIANCE, CODING IS THE ABILITY TO READ AND WRITE A MACHINE LANGUAGE, AS WELL AS THINK COMPUTATIONALLY. LEARNING TO CODE CAN HELP YOU DEVELOP PROBLEM-SOLVING SKILLS, GAIN DIGITAL CONFIDENCE, AND HELP YOU UNDERSTAND THE WORLD AROUND YOU.

FOR MORE INFORMATION ABOUT CODING, VISIT:
WWW.BLACKBOYSCODE.COM
WWW.COLORCODEDKIDS.COM

DID YOU KNOW THERE ARE MANY BENEFITS OF GETTING INTO TECHNOLOGY AND CODING? YOU CAN CREATE YOUR OWN VIDEO GAMES, USE IT AS A CREATIVE OUTLET TO EXPRESS YOURSELF AND EVEN BUILD YOUR OWN WEBSITE. PRETTY COOL, HUH?!

HEY #TEAMTECHBOY! WOULD YOU LIKE TO BE FEATURED IN MY NEXT ISSUE OF TECH BOY?
WELL, HERE'S YOUR CHANCE! TO BE CONSIDERED FOR THIS OPPORTUNITY, CREATE YOUR BEST ORIGINAL SUPERHERO IN THE SPACE BELOW. FOR SUBMISSION, PLEASE UPLOAD YOUR SUPERHERO'S IMAGE TO INSTAGRAM AND TAG ME @TEAMTECHBOY.

DON'T FORGET TO USE THE FOLLOWING CAPTION:
"MY HERO IS A PART OF #TEAMTECHBOY!"

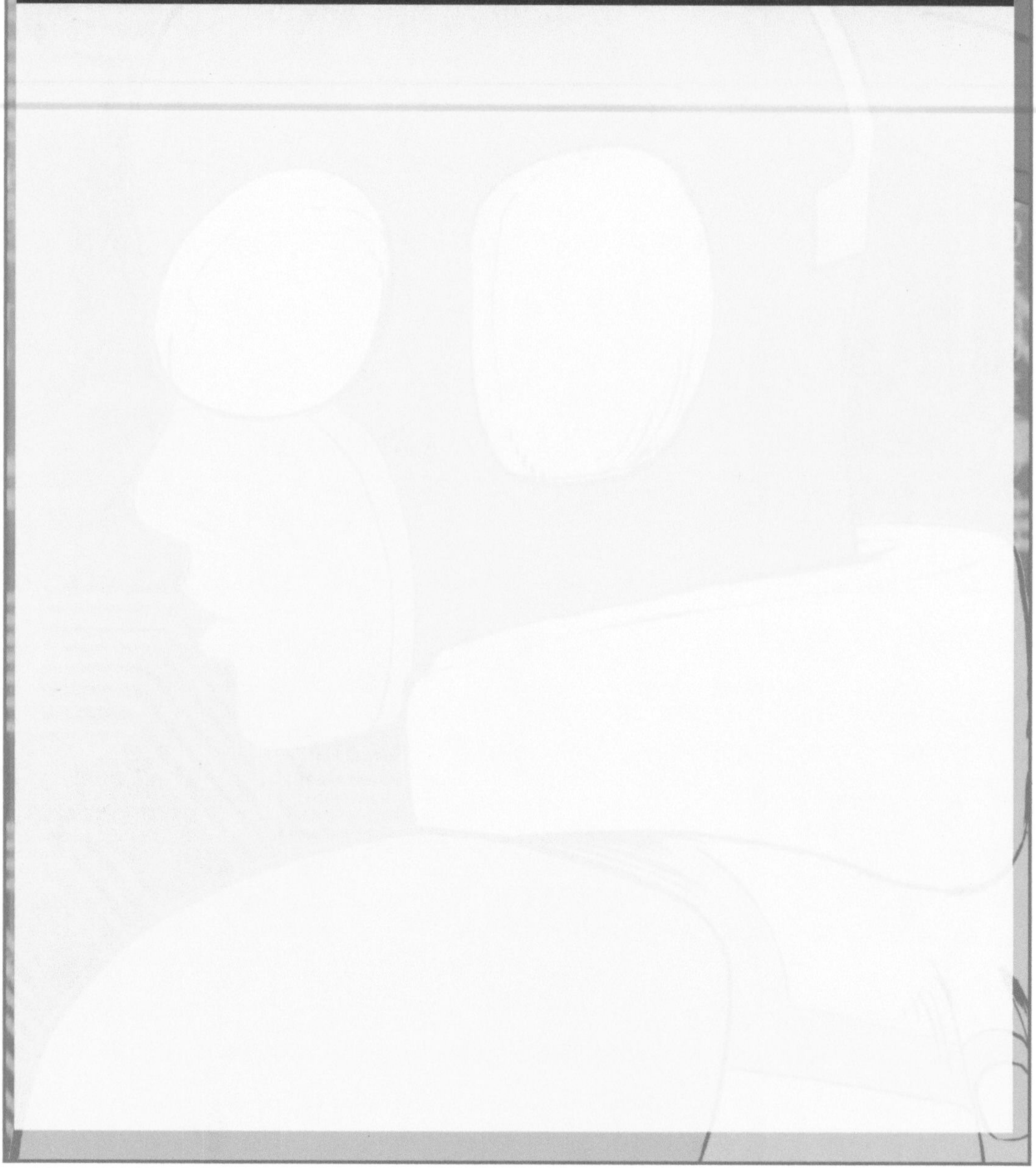

CPSIA information can be obtained
at www.ICGtesting.com
Printed in the USA
LVHW071208200322
713907LV00002B/102